Fable of the Pack-Saddle Child

Praise for *Fable of the Pack-Saddle Child*

Meshing poetry and storytelling, Mia Leonin has created in *Fable of the Pack-Saddle Child* a luminous and mysterious tale about a young girl's search for the meaning of her life. Leonin weaves together the language of the body and the language of the soul in an unforgettable way. Her playfulness with the tilde in Spanish is simply exquisite. Together with stunning illustrations by artist Nereida García Ferraz, this beautiful book will haunt the reader with its evocation of a time and a place halfway between lost dreams and real life.

—Ruth Behar, *Lucky Broken Girl*

Mia Leonin's *Fable of the Pack-Saddle Child* is brimming with the luminous strangeness of nearly pre-linguistic truth born of keen observation, deep feeling, and brilliant imagery. In this haunting, often terrifying hybrid of poetry, dream, fable and magic-spell, Leonin evokes a world that is both absolutely familiar and utterly transformed. *Fable of the Pack-Saddle Child* is a work of sly and surprising power, rich with the sensual fecundity of the real world seen through the eyes of a child's inner life. Its spell will light and lighten our lives.

—Michael Hettich, *The Frozen Harbor*

This tapiz of tales unspools to reveal young Micaela growing up amid "the fables and fibs her mother tells." Not knowing her father, "Micaela wonders what food her father is. Is he scrambled eggs or palomilla steak...?" For simmering below the surface is the story of a girl's budding understanding of the power of language: "*What you have, chiquilla, are words—many, many words.*" So spoke the sage in the gypsy cave. And it's true: all throughout young Micaela's life, it's her garden of palabras that anchors her: "She writes on a fallen palm leaf and the small square of wax paper..." And it's village folk who, seemingly, raise her, including the teacher Señora López, who gifts the girl her first notebook. And slowly *Fable of the Pack-Saddle Child* sneaks up on you as Micaela's unsettling origins are revealed. A category-defying book that movingly marries prose, verse, and image.

—Francisco Aragón, Institute for Latino Studies, University of Notre Dame

Fable of the Pack-Saddle Child

Mia Leonin

Illustrations by Nereida García Ferraz

BkMk Press
University of Missouri-Kansas City
www.umkc.edu/bkmk

BkMk Press
University of Missouri-Kansas City
5101 Rockhill Road
Kansas City, MO 64110

Executive Editor: Robert Stewart
Managing Editor: Ben Furnish
Assistant Managing Editor: Cynthia Beard

Author photo: So-Min Kang

BkMk Press wishes to thank Marie Mayhugh and Jordan Hooper. Special thanks to Dana Sanginari.

Missouri Arts Council
The State of the Arts

Financial support for BkMk Press has been provided by the Missouri Arts Council, a state agency.

Additional support has been provided by the Miller-Mellor Foundation.

Library of Congress Cataloging-in-Publication Data

Names: Leonin, Mia, author. | Ferraz, Nereida García, illustrator.
Title: Fable of the pack-saddle child : poetry / by Mia Leonin ;
    illustrations by Nereida García Ferraz.
Description: Kansas City, MO : BkMk Press, University of Missouri-Kansas
    City, [2018]
Identifiers: LCCN 2017045557 | ISBN 9781943491148 (acid-free paper)
Classification: LCC PS3562.E577 F33 2018 | DDC 811/.54--dc23
LC record available at https://lccn.loc.gov/2017045557

ISBN: 978-1-943491-14-8

This book is set in Constantia.

ACKNOWLEDGMENTS

Many thanks to Ben Furnish, Robert Stewart, Cynthia Beard, and Dana Sanginari of BkMk Press for your patience, diligence, and spirit of adventure.

Collaborating with Nereida García Ferraz was nothing short of transformative. Gracias, Neri! I'm deeply appreciative of your talent, sensitivity, and imagination.

To the early readers of this manuscript—Elizabeth Cerejido, Michael Hettich, and A. Manette Ansay—your encouragement spurred me on.

Shara McCallum read many drafts with insight and enthusiasm. Gracias, hermana. Maureen Seaton, knowing you made this book possible. Love you, Alice!

Gracias mil Ruth Behar and Francisco Aragón.

I am indebted to the Artist in Residence Program at the Deering Estate, where I wrote an early draft of this book.

To my bruja squad – Eva Silot Bravo, Celeste Landeros, Tiffany Madera, and Anne Tschida—mucho aché.

Most of all, much love to my daughter, Rafaela. Te quiero mucho.

Bastard (1642): a derivative from the Old French *fils de bast,* a child conceived on the packs pulled from a horse's saddle and used by travelers as makeshift beds.

—Folk etymology

Morning sputters. Calle Bernardo snakes
along the sea's periphery.

One street over, Micaela walks to school.
She clutches her satchel and comb. She reaches
into her skirt pocket to pinch her lucky opal.

Micaela is a ten-year-old of few miracles:
She can point to a bird and balance a passing plane on her finger.
She's fluent in cat talk and the sign language of trees.
She thinks she can stop her heart by holding her breath.

Micaela's mother's black eyes and hair sparkle when she speaks. Her aquiline nose protrudes unabashedly and big, strong teeth crowd her mouth, giving her the curious beauty of a mare. She possesses few unusual or exceptional talents. She can brew liquor on the stove and from that, whip up an ice cream that requires no churning. She owns one pair of scissors, and, with one blade, she can shave a man's face, poke a hole in a cloudy day, and whistle the "Ave María" through the blade and a piece of paper. All of this she can do with one blade.

Tengo mi manera, Micaela's mother has a way about her. She says so herself, smiling so broadly her red lipstick leaves a half-moon smudge on her front left tooth.

She knows how to talk her way out of eight-days-late rent or the fee on an unpaid electric bill. Men with thick, ruddy fingers pinch her, and she shrieks in mock surprise. The baker tosses an extra empanada into her sack with a wink. The butcher brandishes his carving knife with a gallant's flourish and slices a piece of discounted meat with an extra-wide ribbon of fat. From their street-corner perches, tall, gaunt men circle their hands in the air like magicians when Micaela's mother passes by. She might snatch a bruised apple from a mound of bruised apples and bite into its flesh defiantly or pinch a piece of sweet turrón from the display case, pop the creamy white nougat in her mouth, and belt out a hearty laugh at the vendor, who will inevitably throw up his hands in exaggerated resignation.

Still, Micaela's mother doesn't command the attention of men who own sailboats or men who buy steaks and rubies. She still has to say, *Sí, por favor. Gracias. No pasa nada. We'll be fine.*

On Calle Bernardo, men gape in draping overcoats.
Liver-voiced women snap and bark their wares in the rain.

The neighborhood children steer clear of the former
and are scattered to the street by the latter. Children

form the undigested meaning of each moment.
They chew and chew, sucking the gristle of its fat. They chew,

and pools of hunger well up in their mouths. They pick
at scabbed knees and grow dizzy from the blood scent.

When they smell rain, their incisors ache
to taste the damp earth and clay.

Once, in preparation for a blind date, Micaela's mother sold her great-grandmother's pearl brooch in order to buy one stocking woven from pure Seraphina opaque silk. The entire evening, she waited with one leg on flagrant display and the other naked and crouching beneath the tablecloth like a hungry dog.

Micaela's mother rubs a lipstick back and forth across her lower lip—
four times and then a fifth. She presses her lips together and sings with
the rising melody of a bolero:

¿Que

te

parace

chica?

and then repeats the line, letting each note tumble after the other.

¿Que Te Parece ?

Micaela's mother once traveled to visit a love interest in a distant village that hosts an annual Charlie-Chaplin-look-alike contest. On the train, she painted toothbrush bristles black and glued the moustache to her upper lip. She lined her eyes in kohl and pulled wide-legged wool pants over crimson stockings. Beneath a starched, white, button-down shirt, she draped her breasts in a string of fake pearls. She reasoned that if a man could love her as Chaplin, perhaps he could accept her refusal to bear children.

Micaela and her mother's twin beds face each other on opposite sides of the room. A small table and two chairs separate them. At the far end, an electric burner glows; a cupboard slouches. A narrow, rickety path rattles between their beds like a train car, and a high Roman ceiling ascends toward a molding of delicate laurel leaves. At night, two shoebox-shaped windows blink at Micaela from the upper right-hand corner of the room. When they're alone, Micaela's mother burns candles, and flame-shaped shadows flicker against the walls. She walks between their beds, balancing a votive candle on each upturned palm. She sways her arms and hips like a cobra rising from a cartoon basket. *Micaela*, she laughs, throwing flame-shaped shadows against the walls. *Imagine we are carried through the streets in a candlelit carriage on the shoulders of four strapping Arabs. ¡Imagínate, chica!*

And Micaela imagines it. The four Arabs jostle her with each step. Cymbals and trumpets announce her mother, who dances between candles.

One suitor, a failed-novelist-turned-fisherman who smells of bleach and rubber boots, insists that Micaela's mother listen to a different story every night, but instead of making love to her at the height of each tale, he acts out a shadow play of the story's climax. The result is a spastic display of shapes cast in frightening proportion across the room. Micaela peeks and spies a large, humpbacked shadow inching toward the ceiling. It could fall on her mother like a bag of bricks or swallow her as if she were a minnow in the belly of a whale. Instead, the ascending humpback splinters into ten slimy tentacles. Micaela's mother giggles her bored giggle.

Another suitor works at one of the boutique butcheries tucked behind the wide downtown promenades. He smells of lamb shank, crushed lavender leaves, and a spicy, smoky scent that produces a delightful sneeze. Micaela's mother calls it Arabian mesquite. The butcher to the wealthy bows down and shakes Micaela's hand in robust bursts of energy that pump fresh blood into the small chambers of her heart. The butcher never sits down. He paces the apartment while Micaela's mother pins her curls into an elegant chignon. His fleshy fingers snap to a jazz tune on the radio, cracking like a lion tamer's whip.

On Thursday, there was the butcher's scent and the promise of skirt steak. On Friday, he appeared with a bouquet of lilies from his shop. They aromatize the duck flesh with lily and honeysuckle, he explained to Micaela's mother. Micaela's stomach had done a summersault at this! But alas, there will be no Sunday brunch of cognac-infused chorizo with a soft-boiled, royal Peking duck egg as promised.

The butcher has a butcheress, Micaela's mother quips as she holds up a man's argyle sock matted with dust.

Micaela walks to school. Calle Bernardo snakes along the sea's periphery. She touches the lucky opal that Osvaldo, her favorite among her mother's suitors, once gave her. An amateur geologist and audio bookseller, he explained that the Peruvian opal is special because it contains all colors on the spectrum. *Pero ojo, mi chocherita,* Osvaldo warned as he pinched the tiny stone between his long, pointy fingers, *If you wrap an opal in a bay leaf, you will disappear.*

The ocean wind whistles past, chilling lampposts, babies' noses, and coins. Micaela wears a blue sweater with seashell buttons and her mother's purple scarf wrapped three times around her neck. The fringe of the scarf frays in the wind.

None of the men who visit
the narrow room are Micaela's father.

When she was a baby, he
didn't exist. Now, he's absent.

Micaela's father is the wool coat clipped
from a chipped button,

He is the warm plate swiped
from beneath a cold stew.

He's the zebra
fleeing the stripes' rippled gallop.

He was the *Never was*
in *Once upon a time*.

Now, he's an occasional shiver,
a hard swallow.

Micaela doesn't dare ask who her father really is.
And her mother doesn't dare tell her.

In an abandoned lot, the children play sticks and shields, trampling
the ground under which a looted monastery was long ago buried.

A lemon tree casts sundial shadows, dividing Micaela's arm
into dark and light. She digs a stick into the base of the tree.

Bearing wreathes of torn and tangled leaves,
the neighborhood boys form their armies.

They line up large rocks next to pebbles and yell, *¡Patria!*
With the heels of their ill-fitting shoes, they crush

the pebbles into dust and roar, *¡Rey!*
Their saliva drips into the dust and congeals into a paste

upon which they kick and scream.
They form their armies.

A scrawny, gray cat flops down before Micaela.
He blinks. She nods. She studies him and decides

his kaleidoscope eyes signal good fortune—a trip perhaps
or palm-sized cakes, sprinkled with confectioner's sugar.

From beneath the low canopy of the lemon tree, Micaela
watches the neighborhood boys form their armies.

One is freckled with orange hair. One has a pig's potbelly,
propped up by scrawny arms and legs.

Another has dark, Moorish skin
and the gray eyes of a lizard's underbelly.

Patched together by scabs,
stolen fruit, and sagging socks,

their acrid hunger-breath
keeps stronger enemies at bay.

They thrash their arms
like swords.

Their long, soiled fingernails
curl with a ram's elegance.

They form their armies.

Just a turn of Micaela's head stirs
the lemon tree's lowest branches.

From the womb came a herculean mane
and eyebrows as prominent as hieroglyphs.

And four teeth. Micaela's mother loves
to brag about her wild-haired newborn

who gnawed on licorice bark, day-old bread,
and frozen strips of mango.

Micaela wonders if she was once
a baby bear or a tiger cub.

She imagines herself writhing
on her back, a coconut

clutched between her four paws
or swiping at a hanging vine.

She fancies herself a baby animal
whose mama was swept away by a monsoon.

At night, she strokes the dark hair on her forearm
and asks: *Who was I before I was born?*

The school door opens a crack. Whistles
and giggles, skin slaps and clapping
games pour out.

Señora López's brown wrists brim eternal
against the slate green chalkboard.
In her maple-leaf dress, she recites letters:

Broken circle: *C*
Tie it tight: *O*
Add another: *B*
One leg kicking: *R*

Micaela's dark hair falls in a messy curtain
across her desk. The pink blush of eraser filament
sticks to her sleeping cheek.

Señora López lets her rest, just as she lets others
wash themselves in the school lavatory
or wind toilet paper around their hands like mittens
and slip it into their pockets.

Señora López concentrates on her grading
while the children sneak cold coffee cans
of leftover rice and beans into their satchels.

Micaela prepares high tea for a half circle of dolls.
Her maidens—Maritza, Su Lee, and María—
present her with lemon, lychee, and fig.

The band of laurel around the ceiling blares its trumpets.
Micaela lowers her head with the grace and humility
of a good queen.

Her mother passes by and removes a string of fake pearls.
She squats behind Micaela and pulls her into the perfume cloud
of her long arms and pointy knees.

Looping the long necklace into three strings,
she sits the pearls atop Micaela's head.
Your crown, mi reina, she announces.

Micaela smiles and serves tea without moving her head.
Her arms jut out like a mechanical doll—anything
to steady the crown her mother has made.

Micaela's mother's unrolls white satin gloves to her elbows. She dusts her feet with lavender powder. Her brow bones blare with a trombone gold. Tonight she is going out on the town. She's living it up, having a ball. She's leaving with Rodrigo, sad Rodrigo of the big brown pockets. Micaela ducks out of the way as her mother dashes through the door.

On the day of a failed exam and one scoop of picadillo for lunch
a black stray totters on spindly legs in the direction
of Micaela and her lemon tree.

He sees her and scampers a few feet away.
Micaela doesn't attempt to coax, swaddle, or coo.

She sits motionless until he comes close enough for her
to see the white star emblazoned across his mongrel chest.

She doesn't dare give him a name, but under her breath,
she secretly swallows the article and capitalizes him: *Dog*.

Dog of many masters. Name vanished in sleep,
twitch, growl, and scurry.

Beneath the lemon tree, Micaela and Dog sit three feet apart,
each knowing that joy witnessed is joy snatched away.

Micaela's mother brings home an actor with a trimmed black beard. He comes from an island where he claims women roll tobacco leaves on their thighs and pour rum between their breasts. When he speaks words that end in the letter *s*, Micaela notices that the words go silent like a vulture dipping its beak beneath the ocean's surface. *Cuba!* Micaela's mother says it with surprise and gusto, like when she finds a coin in the pocket of an old dress. Her ruby nails are all aflutter as she ransacks the room and seizes upon a bag of bread scraps Micaela had hidden for Dog. She runs to the bodega downstairs to borrow sugar and a few drops of rum from Doña Nina Sánchez, the grocery lady, to make a bread pudding for the bearded man.

The actor takes note of Micaela without turning his head. He stares at her from the corner of one eye like a fish at market stares from its bed of crushed ice.

Dog doesn't walk Micaela to school
or wag his tail when he sees her.

He scurries from behind trashcans.
He rolls himself into an armadillo shape to sleep.

Dog appears when Micaela sits on the apartment steps
or under the lemon tree in the lot down the street.

When Micaela pulls a bread scrap or a boiled potato from her pocket,
Dog lowers his head, always bowing before receiving a scrap.

He limps to the base of a tree, devours the food, and looks up,
searching for the morsel he no longer remembers.

The bearded man appears another night, and then another. Micaela's mother takes to calling him *the Actor*. *The Actor will return after his show. Let's tidy up. The Actor is coming.* The Actor gets the largest portion of beans and Micaela's fluffy pillow number one. She is left with lumpy pillow number two. Whenever Micaela walks into the room, the Actor raises his eyebrows and lifts his hands as if surprised by her presence.

Doña Nina's tiny bodega smells of strong, sweet coffee and pastelitos. Today, Micaela's mother sent her to buy sugar, and she returned home with salt. Her mother sighs: *¡Ay, mi Micaela está en las nubes! She's day dreamier than ever.* Doña Nina winks at Micaela from behind a stack of newspapers. Her pink and green housecoat, pressed and starched, brushes against the shelves as she paces back and forth, heaving sacks of rice, flour, and sugar onto the shelves.

Doña Nina

One night, the Actor commands Micaela's mother to perform un pase de Verónica over and over, using a bed sheet as the bullfighter's cape. He makes her step back, flip the cape to show the sign of blood and then lunge, withdrawing the cape. *¡Otra vez!* he yells, sitting shirtless on the edge of the bed, one hand balled up and pocketed in the other. *¡Otra vez!* he shouts like a child furious that something delightful is drawing to a close.

But darling, I'm tired. Micaela's mother's voice is as steady as the thumb on a knife slicing potatoes, but in the flick of the sheet Micaela detects a tremor in her mother's hands. The Actor grabs the sheet and snaps it midair. Micaela stares at the crack that runs down the far wall behind her mother's bed. The Actor has turned a simple cotton sheet into a lightning bolt.

Dog's history:

One master stamped out Dog's archeological wag.

        One clipped Dog's tail of its ceremonious flag raising.

One pinched Dog's protective growl into a yelp.

        One master cornered Dog and sat before him as
quiet as a bullfrog.

When Dog twitched,

        he stomped and burst into laughter.

Doña Nina passes by the lemon tree
that has never borne even one fruit.
She examines the lowest branch, rubbing
the wide, glossy leaves between her fingers.
Emerald polka dots pop off her housedress.
She says *hello* through the leaves then pauses:
Micaela, mi cielo. Would you like to sweep up
around the shop in exchange for a bite to eat?

Micaela looks up and squints:
Do you always wear green?

¡Si señorita! Doña Nina laughs.
Stop by the bodega after school.

The Actor slides on imaginary black boots, clicks his heels together, and marches around the room, executing long straight-legged kicks. He shouts with each kick in a language of consonants. The letter *S* clanks against *H* and *K* like the bottles of warm beer Doña Nina keeps underneath the cash register.

From her bed, Micaela watches her mother's profile bristle, but her voice falls from her lips in folds of honey. *Por favor, mi amor. That is Stalin's tongue. For many, it's the language of dictatorship.*

The Actor laughs and swings her in an elegant embrace. *For you, it shall be guaguancó then!* His lean, muscular frame melts into waves and gyrations. He wiggles his hips with a coquettish flair Micaela has only seen women exhibit.

The Actor and Micaela's mother dance and laugh, bumping into the small table that separates the beds. Micaela's mother shrieks with delight as the Actor shouts his kicking language into her neck. Micaela watches their laughter drift up, forming drops of condensation that settle into the ceiling's darkest corner.

A fine scar runs from beneath Señora López's right nostril
to the bow of her upper lip. Whether smiling
or shouting, her mouth twists into a slight sneer.

She strains above the screeching children
and shouts: *Cana Caña.*

Señora López completes the letter:
big *N* with a perfect little *n* above.

One *n* alights atop the other,
like a butterfly on a sleeping nostril.

Micaela sees a little *n* leapfrog atop *Mono*
and land as *Moño.*

A little *n* pops up behind big *N*
and forlorn *Pena* sparkles into *Peña.*

The actor's shadow follows him with a flourish. When he wipes his feet to enter the apartment or snaps the napkin off his lap and drops it on the table, there is his shadow, delighting in his presence, playfully keeping up with him, but almost falling behind. His is a shadow that one feels in the dark. It brushes the backs of Micaela's calves when he walks past her bed to pour himself a glass of water. On sleepless nights, it squats in the corner, daring her to roll over one more time.

I know the character and constitution of each soul
that passes through this doorframe, Doña Nina assures Micaela.

A particular clairvoyance passed down from mother and great-grandmother,
Nina's taste buds water each time she hears a new name.

Just as we each possess a birthstone and an astrological sign,
one singular object of gastronomy reflects each person's soul.

Micaela grins from behind the bins where she's sweeping up
flecks of rice and kernels of dried corn.

Ah ha! Doña Nina's hands emerge from the pockets of her housecoat
like magician wands. *There are those teeth! So you aren't hiding*
a monster in that lovely mouth of yours after all.

Micaela is fried ham—sizzling and salty with a hint of clover honey.
You are thin as a willow switch and unassuming but full of substance,

Doña Nina pinches Micaela's cheek like the doughy corner of an empanada.
Your mother is meringue, she confides. *Whipped up and frilly,*
pretty to look at, but stiff and hard if left alone too long.

Señora López says that in the world of Ñ
for everything large, a smaller part exists.
The children shout out examples:

olive and pit

egg and yolk

pillow and feather

pastelito and crumb

Micaela thinks *mother* and *daughter*.
She draws *ñ* after *ñ*. The dip
and squiggle of her pencil comforts her

like the nights her mother would come home
in a cloud of jasmine and champagne bubbles.
She would climb into Micaela's bed and hold her, molding

Micaela's small body into her long one
as if she were a doll placed high
on a shelf for safekeeping.

Ññ Ññ Ññ Ññ Ññ Ññ Ññ

From across the room, the Actor chatters to no one. Micaela knows her mother is asleep because when she sleeps for real, she makes no breathing sound. The Actor recites a story in the way of actors, swooping in from outside angles and peripheries. He stops occasionally for dramatic effect. *There were fourteen people fleeing at night in a small cigarette boat. A woman traveled alone carrying a book. A priest was also leaving the island, of all things, in search of an Italian woman with whom he'd fallen in love. Everyone aboard begged the priest for his blessing. The woman ripped out the last page of her book . . .*

The Actor's head pops up next to Micaela's. He smells of the rosemary thistle and the pork lard Micaela's mother splurged on for her garbanzo-and-red-pepper stew. His chatter slows to a soft murmur as he slips one hand under the cover of Micaela's narrow bed. Her ear—the one facing the ceiling—is alert like a small sparrow craning to hear a corresponding whistle. The Actor's hand, still and warm, rests on her tailbone. *The woman ripped out the last page of her book,* he whispers. *And just like that she stuffed it in her mouth and began to chew slowly, methodically.* Micaela hears the Actor's jaw pop as he imitates the chewing and moves his thumb to the entrance of her most inside outside part. He eases in his thumb, slick with spit, and shoves it like an eel turned to a wooden broom handle in an instant. Micaela's body shivers and her legs jerk involuntarily, but she doesn't make a sound. The Actor pulls his thumb from her rectum, and a gush of fluid runs down her legs.

When Micaela unclenches her eyes, night has swallowed the Actor. Is he wedged between her back and the wall? Is he crawling toward the foot of her bed? She can't see him, and she can't hear her mother's sleeping breath, the one she feigns to lull her suitors to sleep. Micaela stares in front of her, and when she can finally focus, she catches a glimpse of the dark fish eye staring at her from the other side of the room. The Actor is back in bed, muttering the story of the priest, the boat, and the page-eating woman. Micaela's mother exhales an audible smile in her sleep, *Ay, mi amor,* she sighs, *you and your stories.*

Micaela presses her hand
against a page of smooth white parchment, brushing
and preening the paper.

Her pencil dips and rises.
All around her she sees the curve
that floats above the Ñ.

Señora López notices the trail of tildes inching across Micaela's page

and gives her a special assignment:

Micaela, find the identical words with and without the ñ.
Write what each word means to you.

Señora López's lip curls slightly in a restrained smile.
She peers intensely at a spot on the top of the desk where Micaela stares.

The two appear to examine something diminutive in size,
but of extreme importance.

What do you think? Señora López prods gently.
Micaela shrugs.

Señora López doesn't notice Micaela's left shoulder as it floats
up and lowers, triggering the right shoulder's ascent

Under the lemon tree, Micaela pulls a folded paper from her pocket.
She writes:

Cana

Shock of white hairs.

Caña

Whether stoked by wind or fire, the rustle
of sugar cane stalks sounds the same.

Mono

A playful monkey.

Moño

Before a gasping audience, Micaela
swings perilously high and low.

Slicked back with brilliantine and wound into a tight bun,
her hair glistens like moonlight on ocean waves.

Micaela swings above the crowd. A child grasps
at the breeze as her jeweled toe slips past.

On a sheet of brown butcher paper, Micaela scribbles:

Campana

The church bells ring vespers.

Campaña

She remembers the day she stumbled upon Doña Nina in a crowd,
listening as the mayor promised equal wages.

Every few sentences he withdrew a handkerchief
and wiped his forehead, slick with sweat.

Doña Nina hissed over her shoulder, *¿Que clase de campaña es esa?*
That man's groin simmers to the sound of his own voice.

Micaela sweeps in strokes shaped like ～ ～ ～
Doña Nina hands her a tin bowl, chilled from the icebox.

Micaela gingerly pokes her spoon and sends ripples
through the sweet skin that settles on the boiled milk.
She nearly faints.

Luisa, an older girl with French braids and porcelain skin,
rifles through Doña Nina's candy in five seconds flat.
She turns up her nose and huffs out the door.

Micaela scribbles on a piece of paper sack:

Nata

The heavenly, sweet-scented milk skin.

Ñata

The turned-up-nose girl.

One night Micaela's mother takes an interest in Micaela's dolls. Doña Nina has given her a dark-haired prince in a royal-purple jacket to complete her family. Micaela calls him Prince Miguel. Her mother picks him up by one of his lapels and looks at him curiously.

The Actor is engrossed in a newspaper article, white ash forming at the tip of his cigar. Micaela's mother has been "tango pacing," a habit when she's bored. She walks back and forth across the room in long strides with the flair and showmanship of a tango dancer. *Swish, swish, swish.* She has a way of making one skirt rustle louder than seven petticoats of satin and tulle.

Do you wonder who your father is, mi niña? she smiles in earnest. She pivots on her bare feet, juts out her hip, and taps her index finger just below her eye to let Micaela know she's watching her.

Prince Miguel has just arrived with an armload of plantains and fried fish for María and Su Lee, and a box of chocolates for Maritza. Micaela puts the doll under a pillow and glares at her mother. She is sure that this is one of her tricks, like the time she was going to explain how airplanes work but ended up singing, "Volare."

Micaela's mother glances at the Actor to see if he's listening, but his ears have not perked up.

Chica, you are a pack-saddle child! she declares with an *¡Olé!* stomp and flourish. *I made you from travel, adventure, and dancing. Naciste del viaje, la aventura y el baile.* Micaela stares at Prince Miguel's boot sticking out from under the pillow.

In a midnight milonga, I crept across the dance floor sideways, my long steps as delicate and mysterious as a spider, she whispers, opening her legs with arachnid breadth. *And you were born!*

Timba, regettón, bachata . . . Micaela's mother enunciates each dance by jutting her pelvis in and out with the speed of a snare drum. *And you were born!*

Salsa spun me around and around. In the tradition of my elders, I kept my torso completely still while rocking my hips from side to side. And voilà, you were born!

Micaela's mother whirls around, face flushed, and locks eyes with the Actor, who by now has put down his paper.

¿Tu vez? she boasts. *I too can act!*

The Actor lowers his chin and offers a sarcastic military salute. The white bulb of ash falls to the floor.

Micaela's mother squats in front of the bed to look Micaela in the eye. *I don't know, mi niña*, she whispers, *I danced and here you are.* She grips Micaela's shoulders. Micaela notices Su Lee tossed to the side of the bed in her red ruffle gown as if she too has been dancing all night. Micaela's mother fiercely plants a kiss on her forehead and pushes her back with the conviction of a preacher casting out demons. *You are loved, muñeca. You are loved.* She collapses on the bed next to Micaela and hugs her tightly. Micaela feels the warm sweat from her mother's chest seep into her back. She buries her head in the pillow. A broad smile widens across her face.

Micaela has heard her mother tell too many different stories for any of them to be true. Pack-saddle children are from another time, from a grandmother or great-grandmother's time. Not from this world of cars, trains, busses, and planes. These are the fables and fibs her mother tells when she's entertaining *y la comida está resuelta*—a thin steak smothered in fried onions sizzles in the pan, and warm chianti sloshes over the lip of her jelly jar. When dinner is taken care of and a suitor is there to wrap his arms around her once their bellies are full and Micaela is tucked in. In these moments, Micaela has heard many tales of her birth. Micaela's mother brags about giving birth alone in a stable with a scratchy horsehair blanket under her ass and hay in her hair—*como la virgen*, she always winks.

If Micaela's mother's glass is empty and her companion fails to notice, she might tell the story of her lover the priest, who dropped her off at a neighboring convent to deliver and never again looked her in the eye. Micaela's mother will lean forward on one elbow and hold up her empty glass with an accusatory smile, her small left breast flopping forward like a loose apple dislodged from the heap: *What am I, amor, the priest's lover?* followed by howling laughter and a hearty knee slap.

Once, when everything was turned off for the night, Micaela overheard her mother mumble something to Osvaldo, the Peruvian, something about a stable, a chink of light beaming through wooden planks and shining on a man, a real man, not some holy ghost of a man.

Micaela wonders what food her father is. Is he scrambled eggs or palomilla steak smothered in sweet Vidalia onions? Maybe he's a dessert like arroz con leche o pie de limón. Maybe he's simple and pure—an apple, a tomato, an ear of corn.

Micaela waits for Doña Nina to sample her pot of beans. She wants to slip the question in between Doña Nina's wooden spoon and her lips.

She wants the steam to envelope her question, so that Doña Nina will taste it and speak of her father with the same frankness she uses to announce the quality of the ladle's contents: *Needs salt!* or *This one's for the newspapers!*

What food is my father? Micaela blurts out.

Doña Nina looks up from the spoon suspended in midair: *What has your mother told you about him, child?*

Nothing.

Ask Crab Man, quips Doña Nina, beating the metal ladle against her iron stew pot. *He knows every misfit, malfeasant, and philanderer this town ever shot out its asshole.*

Micaela giggles.

¡Perdóname, mi cielo! Doña Nina's gelatinous arm wiggles as she brings a hand to her mouth. *You're such a good listener; I sometimes forget you're just a little creature.*

Micaela writes on the envelopes of unpaid bills tossed in the trash. She scribbles on a tissue paper that she'd saved because it smelled of rosewater. She writes on a fallen palm leaf and the small square of wax paper from a coconut candy Doña Nina had given her.

She writes:

Maná

Coconut candy

     a double rainbow

          Dog's whiskers brushing her shins.

Maña

to make ice cream with no freezer

     to kill a mouse in one glance

          to turn a living, breathing actor into a wooden puppet.

On a piece of cardboard that Doña Nina let her cut from a used box,

Micaela writes:

Peña Pena

She draws the wide-brimmed sombreros as best she can.
When Señor Lorenzo proposed to Laura, her upstairs neighbor,
a band of red-rose-slinging, trumpet-blaring mariachis
entertained the entire building.

For almost forty minutes the neighborhood was relieved
of its Saturday-night shouting matches and Sunday-morning black eyes.
Even the Actor stirred from his fish bowl of solemnity
for a few minutes of *¡Ole!* and *¡Ay Chihuahua!*

On the back of an old lottery ticket she found stuffed
in a space between the wall and a shelf, Micaela writes:

Nina

   Presto! Doña Nina's round face and cat eyes appear.

Niña

   Doña Nina sprouts pigtails and ribbons.
   The frayed hem of her housecoat shimmers
   into a schoolgirl's plaid jumper.

In the evenings, Micaela's mother keeps the Actor very busy. They rattle the small kitchen table with bottles and glasses. They laugh and stomp until the Actor grows silent and coarse over some stupidity Micaela's mother has uttered. The silence stretches long and taut, then quivers like the wrong chord plucked. Even Micaela can hear it from her cave of sheets and blankets. She opens and closes her fingers like venetian blinds, pretending she can see through the covers.

When she finally peeks out from under, she sees her mother's long pale fingers flowing like sea anemones toward the Actor, who huffs and shoos her away. Micaela's mother soothes his shoulders and the temples of his forehead, talking in one o after the other: *No, mi amor. Mi pobre. No, no. no. No te pongas así.* Micaela aches to be encircled in the bracelets of her mother's o's, to be the object of her long, pale fingers' affection.

She tightens the corners of sheet around her.

In the dark, Micaela traces a tilde in her palm with her forefinger.

A clown's crooked bow tie.

The string of a balloon slipped from a child's hand.

The thread of a hem unraveled.

Micaela wakes to

an earthworm coiling to the touch.

The sleepy waves of her hair in morning's mirror.

~ ~ ~ ~ ~   The vapor that escapes the pot when Doña Nina lifts the lid of her beef stew *for customers only.*

At night Micaela's mother and the Actor make laughing sounds.

And hungry sounds.

Micaela pours red and black beans into separate bins.
Dog suns himself on the lowest step of the bodega.

Neighbors poke their heads through the narrow doorframe
to buy a pack of cigarettes or a sack of flour.

Buenas. ¡Pasen, pasen, por favor! They smile
in response to Doña Nina's prompt greeting.

Occasionally an old man will lift his hat
and exclaim: *You looks good today, mamacita!*

Doña Nina cackles, brushing away the compliment with one hand
and pressing out the mint-green leaves of her housecoat with the other.

Micaela thinks she'd like to have her own bodega someday.
She will sell dulce de leche, Chiclets, and pastelitos de guava y queso.

People will smile at her from the doorway and say *hello*.
She and Dog will smile from behind the counter.

Micaela follows the blue-skinned man to his perch in front of the cathedral by the sea where Calle Bernardo meets Avenida Aragón. The neighbors call him *Crab Man* because of his arthritic waddle.

Micaela stands on the opposite corner as Crab Man arranges himself in the shade of the church. He sits on a concrete block and indeed, from afar, his large belly casts an ecru sheen, and his short, stubby arms and legs splay outward with crustacean stiffness. Crab Man flicks his pinchers in Micaela's direction, so she shuffles toward him, letting the soles of her sandals smack against the street and reverberate off the church walls.

Who is my father? she blurts out.

Crab Man smiles, and as his shiny, rotund cheeks rise, his pupils sink out of view like two black tugboats dipping below the horizon. He holds out his hand, palm facing down, and drops something in her hand. *This is all you need to know,* he declares. The shell feels like a coin in her palm. She examines it closely. The coral ridges make a ~ ~ ~ ~ ~ pattern across the fan of the shell. *One thousand years ago, the waves imprinted their muffled cries on the shell that now fits neatly in your hand,* Crab Man informs her in a flat voice.

Hmmph! Micaela slips the shell in her pocket, turns on her heel, and leaves.

The Actor has been gone for days. Micaela's mother is at the kitchen table arranging daisies, which means she thinks he will return soon. The crack in the wall whittles into an ever-thinning black line. Micaela observes the lonely curve winnowing its way beneath her mother's bed.

It comes to mind one day when Micaela's mother happens upon the messy pages of her daughter's odd homework. Words like *cabana* and *cabaña* are scribbled on the backside of a playbill the Actor brought home from one of his performances in the north. The words are framed by endless rows of

And in the lower right-hand corner, the words *cono* and *coño*. Next to the latter, Micaela has drawn an angry face to underscore *coño* as an expletive.

As a fifteen-year-old girl, Micaela's mother had similarly understood the word *coño* as a harmless curse word shouted or muttered by adults at every domestic mishap. *¡Coño!* for the plate broken or a cake dropped. *¡Coño!* when the electricity went out in the middle of the telenovela. *¡Coño!* for the soup that's too thin. *¡Coño!* for the thread evading the needle's eye.

It comes to mind one day, then it leaves.

Micaela's mother grew up in a small farming village in the center of the country. So far from the ocean, she'd never tasted sea foam or slept to the sound of the waves. Micaela's mother knew nothing of bachata or guaguancó. She knew boiling water for baths, slapping laundry across wide, flat, creek stones, and stirring a pot over a wood-burning stove until every fiber of her dress smelled of slash pine and cordwood.

Micaela's mother's family had travelled to town, and she stayed to keep an eye on the hens and their chicks. It was late afternoon when the cousin of an uncle's friend suddenly towered in the doorframe of the chicken coop. He'd never looked, leered, or even smiled at her, but there in the last shaft of afternoon light and the thrumming of the hen's throats, he pounced. In a thrashing gesture, he yanked off her underwear and fell upon her. First he lurched and missed. Then he cursed and spit, and the cursing made him strong, and what was strong in him, he pushed into her.

Coño, coño, coño the uncle's friend's cousin stammered as he sawed into Micaela's mother, and with his last push, he cried out, *¡Coño divino!* and the harmless household expletive became a noun, *her* noun, the only noun she'd ever vowed to protect. She'd promised in her white veil and gloves. She'd promised before the entire village in a procession of seventeen girls and boys.

With one thrust and one word, *divino*, Micaela's mother was hurled across the equator of maidenhood into motherhood. The last shaft of light vanished. The needles of the longleaf pine out back turned silver. The uncle's friend's cousin wept, and what was strong in Micaela's mother grew round and stronger than her.

Three weeks after the birth, Micaela's mother's body deflated to its previous shape, never again to grow round or to reveal even the slightest stretch or sag. Three weeks after that, Micaela was a sturdy package. Her mother changed from her black clothes to a borrowed violet dress. She washed the incense and litanies from her hair, wrapped Micaela in a blanket like a tamale, and dropped her into the deep cotton hammock of her shawl. With Micaela in the crook of one arm and a suitcase beneath the other, she marched off to the nearest distant city, never to return. Her enormous family was too hungry and too disgraced to be anything but relieved.

The first thing Micaela's mother did in the city was to find someone to make her smile, or did she make him smile? Either way, it didn't matter. The smile was the thing. As she hobbled down Calle Bernardo, exhausted from the long bus ride and in search of a room to rent, a man on a red bicycle pedaled by slowly. He pulled a small wagon and blew on a kazoo that was attached to a string around his neck. Occasionally, he called out: *Plastics, glass, newspaper, and metals! I collect all things old and used!* As he passed by, Micaela's mother drew the baby up from the dark well of her shawl and offered the man a glimpse at Micaela's fresh face.

Without her, I think I might be material for your wagon, she joked.

The man shook a scolding finger at her: *Señorita, you are as lovely as the day is long!*

Or as lovely as the least ugly thing thrown out, she quipped.

They both laughed, and the man pedaled on, stoutly blowing his kazoo. Calle Bernardo bustled with dusty kids scrambling to play, fruit sellers unpacking crates, and fishermen lugging traps and bait. Micaela's mother noted how readily people smiled in the city, unlike the somber village folk. She swore never again to keep her body sacred. In this new city, her body would be an instrument of laughter, joy, and pleasure. This was her new vow.

Beneath the lemon tree, the boys poke
at Micaela with their sticks. They have come
to claim Dog, wild-eyed and snarling
from behind Micaela's torso.
She knew this day would come. She reaches
into her pocket. Her fingers brush
against her seashell and lucky opal. She fumbles
for a rusted fish hook she found on the way to school.
She wills it to grow larger and land
in the ear of her attacker, but it feels
as small and harmless as a hangnail.

The boys toss her out of the way.
They circle Dog. They have wanted
an enemy for their war games,
and Dog will suffice.
He growls and snarls. His lame leg
quivers, and the hair stands up
on his bony frame.

The boys kick and kick. They look
directly at Dog and howl.
Only the chubby redhead clenches
his eyes shut. His face is contorted
as if he's the one being kicked. Micaela hates
him even more than the others. She stumbles
across the street. She shakes her fist and screams
at the redhead.

Because an animal can't shield himself
in a self-protective stance, Dog
topples over when he can no longer stand.
A gelatinous eye stares out from his immobile carcass.

The boys kick long after Dog has yelped
his final yelp. They kick until Dog
is a bumpy patch of black. They kick
until he is a pelt, trampled
into the dust.

Down the street at the gravel pit just outside the market, Micaela's mother's strong legs and strappy golden sandals plant narrow holes in the ground. She's just purchased garbanzos and sweet potatoes, and she watches Micaela's skinny frame jump up and down, excitedly punching her small fist toward the sky. As with any parent, it surprises her to see an unfamiliar gesture inhabit her child's body. She is pleased and relieved to see shy Micaela cheer on the neighborhood children's game.

At school, Micaela grows sleepier and sleepier. She wakes and scribbles

The buckle on her shoe.

A wing in search of its twin.

The snail's trail of slime.

Micaela fishes it from her hand

a slug inching

a snake slithering

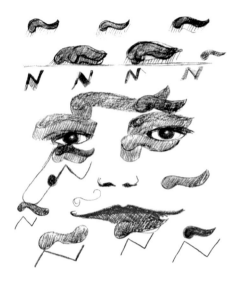

Micaela pushes the broom across the floor in ⁓ shaped strokes. Doña Nina hears the child intone *Ña Ña Ña* in time with the broom's brush strokes. She sees her draw squiggly lines on the tops of dusty cans before wiping them clean.

¿Estás bien, cariño?

Micaela nods.

What song are you singing? Can I join in? Doña Nina hums, flutters, and belts out all sorts of tunes, thinking the girl has taken an interest in singing, but Micaela shakes her head *no*, almost embarrassed.

Micaela places the scraps of papers and leaves
into one of her mother's old shoeboxes.
On the lid, she draws her face. She gives herself
a crown and a necklace of ～ ～ ～

Micaela has never envied the black-lace mantillas of the widows
who duck under the cathedral door every day at noon,
nor the heavy, jeweled metal of Queen Isabella's tiara.

The crown hovers slightly above her like light.
A slight piece of string dangles just above her right ear, the last glimpse
of a balloon that's drifted away with the Actor's face sketched inside
and stretched into a grimace.

Micaela shuffles down Calle Bernardo touching the opal in her front pocket. Its electric-blue striations thrum beneath her fingertips. In her back pocket, a bay leaf nestles like an unopened letter. She is considering disappearing, but she has questions:

Can she separate the opal and bay leaf and become visible again?

Can she touch material items once she's invisible?

Will she have hunger and thirst?

Can she speak to others who have disappeared?

Can she pet them?

Micaela gives Señora López her shoebox of *Ñ* words. She hands over the box of papers, palm leaves, and playbills. Señora López takes it carefully and smiles her twisted smile. *Thank you, Micaela. I will put this in a safe place under my desk for now.*

The day returns to the *click click click* of abacus beads.

On her saint's day, Micaela finds a little bag of candied almonds and a card drawn by her mother under her pillow.

Micaela stares at the tildes scripted in her mother's florid style, the bosomy heart, its left ventricle more inflated than the right. In one hand-drawn heart, she sees all the tildes that have been her secret for the last few weeks.

Micaela remembers all the ～ shaped giggles she had shaken from her arm and how on walks to school her neck had stretched at least four centimeters to meet the ～ ～ crown that hovered above her, how one day a group of classmates had noticed her new walk and burst out laughing. *¡Monga!* they had screamed in a fit of hysteria.

In black ink Micaela carved the word *ano*
onto a black piece of paper.
Just writing it once, she felt
the leaking place.

She'd always known the correct name
for all her parts.
Her mother insisted.

Beneath *ano*, she wrote *año*.
And she wrote it again.
And again. *año año año año año año año año año año año año*

until it made a tower of years around her and the most outside of her
inside place.

año año
año año
año año
año año
año año
año año
año año
año año
año año

Micaela pressed a black crayon to the black paper and rubbed
back and forth over the words. She scrubbed,

but through the waxy flecks of crayon
the leaky word still shone.

Micaela stares at the card her mother made her. Her bed creaks. Micaela's mother sits on the edge of the bed opposite her, smiling and expectant. The Actor has urged her to find out *What's in that child's head* and make a game of it or something lovely, and she's proud of her powers of observation.

Micaela's eyes water. The bed creaks as she shifts her weight. She feels nauseous, out to sea, past Crab Man and the fishermen—their traps set, their eyes wrinkled shut. She slouches and folds her arms across her sunken chest to stop the waves of nausea. She's floating and just on the horizon, she spots a buoy with a wreath of lilies and yellow roses. She imagines Dog buried at sea. His body carried in a golden box past the cathedral, the neighborhood women orating under their breath. He is put out to sea with his favorite foods—pistachios and boiled sweet potato. Micaela clutches the card and cries.

¿Pero, que te pasa, chica? her mother snaps. *Why would you cry over a bag of candy?* Her anger melts into an expression of concern, but she doesn't move, not even once Micaela has scrambled to her feet and run out the door, leaving the card in shreds on her bed. The crack in the wall dives downward and disappears.

Señora López opens Micaela's box and peruses its items, picking up each wrapper, square of paper, and leaf to see what is written there. The black page surfaces, and a wave of dread rolls through her gut like stumbling across a gun or a dead animal.

Señora López

One last ~ takes shape before Micaela's eyes and she must follow it.

Busses rumble toward downtown. Crates slide and fall from the backs of trucks. Evening settles, and the sea smells like the rainbow slick of gasoline as the outboard motors of small boats shut off for the day. The busses careen around cobblestone corners toward the main boulevard that leads downtown. On Calle Bernardo stevedores change from work boots into soft leather loafers. Women call their children to help with dinner or send them to the corner for an extra onion or bag of breadcrumbs. Micaela has followed the ∼ shaped smoke to the back of a bus, through downtown, and then up a steep hill toward the gypsy caves. The ∼ ∼ ∼ is not the cherry-scented cigar smoke of the men who play dominos outside cafés and wear pressed handkerchiefs in the pockets of their mended shirts. This smoke is of peppered goulash and tripe. Even though she's only heard of them, Micaela knows this is the smoke that leads to the gypsy caves on the steep side of a hill at the edge of the city.

Micaela has heard only stories of folly and doom at the gypsy caves. In the gypsy cave floats the last breath of every baby who never woke up, the money of every unfortunate soul who gambled away his family's savings, the eloquent essays and complex computations of every child born dumb, the howl in the pants of every man who walks away from his family. Even the barrio's most conniving, thieving, cheating citizens will say it: *Nothing good can come from the gypsy caves.*

Micaela climbs up a brick path that turns to gravel and then winds into dirt. Along the way, fat gray women hold out sprigs of rosemary to her. If you take the rosemary, they will tell your future, and if they tell you the future, you owe them money. Micaela's ankle boots crunch hexes into the dirt, and she looks down to ignore the sprigs of truth poking at her. She once reached out and took one, and her mother screeched, swooped down, snatched it, and threw it at the gypsy woman who muttered a foul-sounding curse in a foreign tongue. She slapped Micaela, then shook out her hand as if it were on fire. *Chica! Don't ever take anything from a gypsy—least of all your future.*

Lately, Micaela has lost the sound of her own footsteps. She feels herself wafting through her days like the ∿ shaped smoke she now follows. Even without joining opal and bay leaf she is vanishing. For this reason, she's not afraid to walk up the steep hill to the gypsy caves. The closer she gets, the more she hears her own sounds—the gurgle of her belly, and yes, the crunch of her long, narrow foot soles. Perhaps it's a good sign.

As Micaela approaches the mouth of a cave, she comes upon a large man lolling on his side near a small fire. A bright yellow daisy peeks through the buttonhole on the lapel of his dusty suit. He strums a three-stringed guitar and smokes shisha. Micaela stands in front of the fire and watches the flames waver, barely lighting up the mouth of the cave. A young skinny woman kneels, holding a pan over the fire with a long pair of blackened brass tongs. Micaela thinks she looks like a teenager, but her countenance is so stern (unlike the silly, giggling bigger girls of Micaela's neighborhood), she decides she must be a young mother. The woman stares ahead, sucking in her lower lip and pushing it out. Micaela waits. The young woman reels in the tin pan, takes a couple of listless bites of beans, and stands next to her. Her hair smells of cooking and sage, but when she opens her mouth to speak, a strong whiff of something antiseptic overwhelms Micaela's senses. For the first time, she feels a pang of fear.

What do you have for me, chiquilla? the woman grunts.

Micaela doesn't reach for her pockets. She has no coins, only the seashell Crab Man gave her in her left pocket and the Peruvian opal in her right. The gypsy woman smiles as her hand snakes gently into Micaela's right hand pocket. She retrieves the opal and holds it up.

¿Está bien, chiquilla?

Micaela nods, sacrificing her opal to the gypsy woman. A bubbling sound gurgles from the man's pipe, and her stomach growls in response.

Open your mouth. Abre.

Micaela looks at the bearlike man lolling about with his long, elegant pipe.

¡Abre! the woman repeats.

Micaela opens wide, and the gypsy woman peers inside and mumbles under her breath *Abre, Abre, Abre* like the dentist does when he pokes his pointy metal tools at one particular tooth.

You have no voice, no lengua, no langue, no language, no tongue, she whispers, her words echoing as if she were somehow speaking from inside Micaela's mouth. She takes a small step back and looks Micaela in the eye. *What you have, chiquilla, are words—many, many words.* She touches the bottom of Micaela's chin, signaling her to close her mouth. *There are many stories in you, but you don't know any of them.*

The woman bends over and offers the pan of beans to the man who is now strumming his guitar of three strings. He juts his chin toward the ground, and she places the pan next to his foot. She ducks into the cave and disappears.

Micaela turns to leave. From the big, serene, bear-like man comes a deep, sorrowful canto. It trembles in Micaela's chest. He sings in his native tongue and claps his hands, which sound like dozens of teaspoons tapping. His song makes anything of value feel very, very, very far away. When she catches her balance from shuffling and sliding down the gravelly hill, and she's made the turn back toward her barrio away from downtown, Micaela thrusts her cold hands into her dress pockets and discovers the Peruvian opal joined with her seashell. Crab man had told Micaela that the whorl of every shell turns clockwise. She takes out the shell and runs her fingers across its coral ridges. Just then she realizes that Crab Man gave her a shell whose whorl runs counter-clockwise. In her other pocket, she discovers a card with a white hand grasping a sword. A wreath and a crown balance at the tip of the sword. She returns the card to her pocket and heads home.

Señora López smiles her kind, upturned-lip smile
when she returns Micaela's box of *N* and *Ñ* words.

She's placed a small square package wrapped in butcher's paper
among the penas and peñas, the conos and coños, the manás and mañas.

Micaela goes to the lemon tree to open the package.

Not the tree's leaves, but the branch itself
emits the slightest scent of citron.

She unwraps the gift for several minutes, all ten fingers
congregate at each taped corner to pry open the package.

Inside, she finds a blank book with a persimmon-red cover.
Señora López has written:

Now you can write your other letters.

Micaela smoothes out the first page,
brushing it over and over.

On a wooden stake Micaela writes:

D
O
G

Below this she glues the card of swords and marches to the abandoned lot where she kneels and plants the stake at the foot of the lemon tree.

She looks straight ahead at the boys, who now play soccer with a donated ball and black pads for their knees. She knows they're watching from their periphery of shouts and whistles.

The next day, where Micaela planted her stake in the ground, neighbors have placed smooth river stones, a handful of marbles, and a chain of purple wildflowers. Micaela reaches in her pocket and drops her opal, bay leaf, and seashell among the offerings.

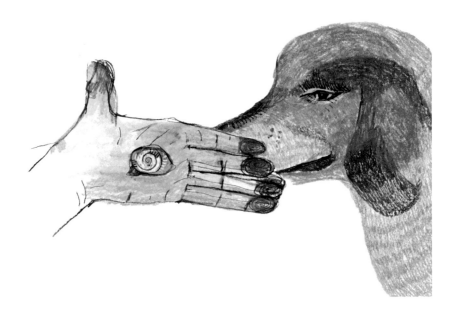

Epilogue:

In the bodega, Micaela sings with Doña Nina, old boleros about broken love wrapped up in new handkerchiefs. Micaela does not have the voice of an angel or the voice of someone whose harmonies can make the most stoic couples cry. She does not have a voice that compels people to stand closer. Micaela has the voice of someone who loves to sing. It rises high and crashes low like a kite in rough winds. It may not soar, but it swoons. It may not cry for help, but it warns. Its whisper just might stop a toddler from waddling into the street. It might lure a kitten from inside an engine or coax a wobbly puppy from a wolf's stare.

Micaela's voice lilts, then lifts off. It ruffles the sheets sagging on rooftops. It cools scorched foreheads. It sweeps through Calle Bernardo, massaging every stray cat's ears, rubbing every missing dog's belly.

Mia Leonin is the author of three previous collections of poetry: *Chance Born, Unraveling the Bed,* and *Braid* (Anhinga Press) and a memoir, *Havana and Other Missing Fathers* (University of Arizona Press). Her poetry and creative nonfiction have been published in *New Letters, Prairie Schooner, Alaska Quarterly Review, Indiana Review, Witness, North American Review, Guernica,* and others. She has  written extensively about theater and culture for the *Miami Herald, New Times, ArtburstMiami.com,* and other publications. Leonin teaches creative writing at the University of Miami and lives in Miami, Florida.

Nereida García Ferraz is a Cuban-born artist based in Miami, whose practice encompasses painting, photography, video, sculpture, and social art projects. Her works have been exhibited widely in the United States and abroad in such venues as the Miami Dade College Museum of Art and Design, the Museum of Contemporary Art in Chicago, Museo Universitario del Chopo and Museo de Arte Moderno in Mexico City, Forms of Contemporary Illinois at Illinois State Museum, and Islip Art Museum, NY.